The Words in my Head

Carla De Villiers

BookLeaf Publishing

India | USA | UK

Presentation by *BookLeaf Publishing*

Web: www.bookleafpub.com

E-mail: info@bookleafpub.com

ISBN: 9789357446334

First edition 2022

ACKNOWLEDGEMENT

Thanks to Catherine Haworth, a close friend who got me back into writing after a many-yeared break, who recommended this poetry challenge to me, and who has been a great support.

And of course, special thanks to Ajax and Achilles, for brightening up my days.

The First of December

As the day comes around again,
Again I watch, a passenger in my memory
As my trembling hands push down
On your chest.
I call out the beat
From the woman on the phone:
Now…now…now…
Down…down…down…
Into the depths.
I choke along with you,
Shove my fingers in your mouth
To push down your treacherous tongue
As it swells to block your throat.
The sound of sputtering,
Of your struggling airways failing,
Is the background noise
That lurks behind my thoughts.
The starlight in your eyes
Fades bit by bit
Dulling as your spirit
Turns from me.
In the moment I am numb

But now I watch with dawning dread
As I fail you, again, and again, and again.
The truest horror
Is the one that sits in your soul,
That you carry in your chest,
Crouching in your breast.
I reel with the shock
As you die a second death
…and a third
…and a fourth.
My lungs twist,
I hold my breath
To hold in the keening rip of regret
As I remember your face
With the bulging eyes
And the mounting dread
As your stiff body lies
Before me.
Each year I set aside this day
As my mind runs rampant
And grief digs deep
Its roots poisoning the well
And trapping me in this labyrinth
To run from the minotaur of guilt
And relive the day endlessly
That I let you down.
And when the long night passes I wake
And escape
And block the door behind me.

Until next year
I live in fear
Of your face appearing in my dreams
And the sound of choking
Sends me into a spiral.
I'll see you again
At the end.
And every day until then.
Let me go.
I can't let you go.

Hiding Inside

You don't know me
The way you think you do.
The whimper that I carry inside,
The flinches I try to hide,
The gossamer threads that tie me down…
Down…
Down…
Into the belly of the beast,
Where we keep out of sight
Of the ghosts that roam the night,
And clasp hands over our mouths
To muffle the breathing and the screaming
And the waking, and the aching
And the wishing we were dead.
This hole inside my head
Where corpses do not lie
And the living do not die,
No matter how they try.
I long to let it go,
The echoes from within.
But it's too late, I know.
I cannot let you in.

Your Body Isn't Yours

Your body isn't your own.
It belongs to the man down the street
Who shouts 'get yer tits out'
At the schoolgirls walking by,
Laughing awkwardly to fill
The uncomfortable silence that they don't yet
know how to deal with.
And to the middle-aged men,
Family friends
That pull them in for a squeeze
And a kiss on the cheek,
The saccharine sweet
Disgust you can't show.
And to the guys in the club
Who watch as you dance,
And sneak up behind
To grind against you
And slip hands up your skirt
And curse when you push them away,
Flushed and afraid.
And to the boyfriends who came with
Valentines' flowers,

The currency they pay
To have you any which way
And you don't get a say;
You owe them this.
And to the friend that walks you home
After a long night of partying
And invites himself in
And before you can begin
To realise
He is pressing you down, inside
And out. Ignoring your cries
And forcing the fight
Out of you.
To leave you broken and bleeding
And shivering with shame
Because you're the one to blame.
And to all the other men
That hear the stories and say
That it isn't a problem that most of us face.
That you read too far into it
And say, why, he's a nice guy.
He wouldn't hurt a fly.
And that's fine, but you're not a fly or a flea.
You're me.
And I'm you.
And we'll get through this.

Don't Touch Me

Don't touch me.
I burn and shake and shiver.
Fear scratches the surface of my skin
Where your scent lingers,
Carving obscenities into my soul.
I simmer
With suppressed screams,
Broken trust,
And broken dreams.
Don't touch me.
My breath comes short and shallow and sharp.
The weight of blame
Settles on my shoulders
Like the weight of your body
Pressed into mine.
I suffocate in silence
As sobs stick in my stomach.
The sick confusion
Of where you end and the pain begins.
The waiting haunts me.
Let it end or let me.
Don't touch me.
I choke through the collar of bruises,
The hot, heavy breath
Burns with the bile in my throat.

The steady rhythm
Matches the hammering of my heart.
Let me out, let me out,
Let it leap from my chest
And leave me to rest.
Don't touch me.
Shame bends my spine
And bows my head
And twists my mind
And breaks my bed.
I clench my teeth
And whimper,
My shoulders shudder
As I whisper
Don't touch me.

Branded

You leave bruises on my body like brands.
I am nothing to you.
Your hands
Descend upon me.
I grow bitter with bile,
I simmer and rage,
I flinch at your smile
And this war that you wage
Against me.
Once more, the hand comes down,
The fist, the stick
The pain that licks
Across my spine
To teach me manners
Or rather,
To teach me silence.
I sit and wait.
You taught me obedience
And you taught me hate.
I bide my time
As you take mine.
I count the days
And count the ways
To leave you behind.
But still I hang on for one kind word,

For one pleased smile
Anything to make me feel worthwhile,
Starving and desperate,
I live for those moments
And loathe you for them.
The bitter truth
Is that I need you
And you know it too.

Medusa's Cry

I stare at the mirror, at what I've become.
A desiccated husk of what it means to be a
person,
Withered beyond all recognition.
I taste you in the burning at the back of my
throat,
In the salt tracks that weather my cheeks,
Carving our story into my flesh,
The words I detest
Turning ash upon my tongue,
Ringing in my ears.
I am left
Mute and deaf,
Staring wide eyed as you walk on by.
They say love is blind
But tell that to the memories fixed in my mind,
The faces I see when I close my eyes,
The hot, hard lump in my throat I despise.
I grind my teeth to dust,
Feel my jaws crack under the pressure,
Snarl toothlessly through bleeding gums,
Spit blood at your feet as you pass me.
I slither towards you, watch you cry out in fear.
Whisper Medusa and watch me stumble.
I laugh, or cry,

Remind me what the difference is?
Watch now as the life dries in your eyes.
I weep dust and cry,
Why.

The Waiting Widow

Day in, day out, I stare out the window,
Watching days pass by
As I wonder why
Has no one come for me?
Did they forget?
The clock ticks on
As the sand empties in my hourglass,
Each grain one by one
And still I sit alone.
My ribs stick through my skin,
Paper thin,
The tracery of veins
A map of the world's rivers,
Places I long to see.
I long to be
But I rot,
Stuck in the stagnation of age,
The miserable swamp
From which I will never again rise.
The wheeled chair
A torture device.
These gnarled fingers,
A stranger's hands.
The withered reflection
I can't understand

Where have you gone?
It's been so long.
And still the waiting
Goes on and on.
I dream of my life,
The day-to-day things
That I took for granted.
The people
That have left me behind.
I worry that when you do come
You'll find
An emptiness where once my mind
Flourished.
For now, I stare out the window,
Watching days pass by
And I wonder why
Has no one come for me?

Leviathan

I see you with her and burn,
Seething and sore as I bare my teeth
And clench hands into fists,
Nails needling into palms.
Poison shivers down my spine
And taints my mind
As I feel the roar of that monster inside.
Leviathan rises in the deep dark waters of my
chest
And lashes out in my breast
Sending waves to destroy
The little I had left.
Murky green tendrils cloud my vision,
Colour you in hues of sea glass
Swimming just out of reach
While I drown, dragged down
By the anchor I have found
And cannot let go of.

Broken Down

I stare you down,
The distance between us profound,
As you speak the words I never thought would
come.
I curse you with words like lead
But only inside my head.
As I turn to stone
The loneliness in my bones
Leaves me frozen and fossilised.
Numb though I hurt.
I pretend I haven't heard.
Love is a dirty word.
And an insidious poison,
The leech on your mind
That leaves you blind.
You leave me behind,
And leave me to choke
On the festering remains
Of what was once hope.
And now it's taking too long.
Please just get on
With it.

Little Red

I slip between the trees,
Searching in the dark,
Eyes drinking in the moonlight
That lights the forest path.
Here, I will face my love,
My heart full and fast,
Breathing in excited gasps
As we near at last.
I smile shyly to myself,
Feel the nervousness start,
How keen is my soul,
How eager my heart.
I feel you close by
And the knowledge warms my skin.
I breathe a soft sigh
And smiling lift my chin
To wash my face in starlight
As I imagine your hand upon my cheek,
Your lips touching mine,
Our bodies entwined.
And as we embrace
In the silvered light
The look on your face
Is the most perfect sight,
The love of my life.

I watch the passion play in your eyes
As I whisper,
Hi.
*

I slip between the trees
Searching in the dark
Scenting eagerly at the air
As I hunt my mark.
Here, I will face my prey,
My heart full and fast,
Breathing in excited gasps
As we near at last.
I grin around my fangs,
How well I've played my part.
How sharp are my teeth,
How hungry my heart.
I feel you close by,
The heat of triumph warms my skin
And the sound of your sigh
Excites my sin.
I dream of sinking my teeth
Into the ripeness of your neck,
And ripping
And ripping
And as we fight,
In the dying night,
The look on your face
Is the last glint of light
As the sunset dies.

I watch the struggle seep from your eyes
As I whisper,
Goodbye.

Expectations

Don't do this I scream
As I wake from the dream,
Panting and obscene.
I cradle myself,
The horror rising in my chest,
Clawing through my ribs,
The nausea I suppress.
Their words ring in my ears:
You might change your mind.
You're too young to decide.
Won't your husband mind?
Because my body is an incubator
And I am just a vessel.
I shiver in disgust. I'll die if I must.
Just let me be my own
And leave me alone.

The Heart Surgeon

I am inside you
Wrist deep
As you lay there asleep
Under the glare
Of the surgeon's light.
Ribs yawning open,
The pulse of your heartbeat shivering inside.
The sight so profane
As I watch it all strain
Against me.
I loop the thread through
And pull on it tight
And even then, you
Are powerless to
Try to fight.
I watch you wake, groggy and confused,
Limbs clumsy with anaesthetic,
That animal instinct driving you
To scrabble awkwardly,
Oblivious to
My face above,
Watching you recover,
In fits and in starts,
After breaking your heart.

Fear is a Prison

The door gapes before me,
Black and shut firm.
I hesitate at the handle.
Turn back to you, stomach clenching,
Fingers twitching to reach for you
And pull you close
And never let you go.
I swallow past the hard knot in my throat,
Refusing to choke,
And turn to leave.
But the maggots of doubt
Wriggle in my mind
And I can't shut it out,
These thoughts and the blind
Panic.
I thrust through the door, panting and weak.
You're okay, you're okay.
I'm okay.
I hold you tight as the fear leaks
From me
And becomes relief,
And that sick sense of grief
Loosens in my throat.
And I turn back to the door,
Black and shut firm,
And lock it.

The Gardener

The soil is rich and soft beneath her hands
Darkening her palms as she digs in the soft loam
Each careful scoop gently placed aside.
A patient row of perfect pits
Appears before her as she sits
The sun warming her back,
Smiling down on her.
In each hole she places a bulb,
Tamping down the soil with slow, firm presses,
Both hands spread,
Working through the flower bed.
As the sun dips her sleepy head low in the sky
She gives a satisfied sigh,
And leaves her garden behind.
Mornings dawn and evenings set
As she keeps the soil tended and wet
And at last, movement,
A tiny green wriggling of life worming from the
earth,
Beautiful in its vibrant defiance,
The green so bright it aches the eyes.
Dawn by dawn she arrives to coax the tendrils
Upwards, up,
To share the sunlight with her freckles
And the sunburnt tip of her nose.

She wipes the sweat from her brow,
Rolls shoulders stiff from crouching,
And smiles down at the world she has built.
Tenderly she untangles the stems coiling about,
Pulling a few out.
Removing the questing creepers
That threaten to take over,
And leaving her plants free to sway in the wind,
Leaves rustling in the breeze.
Dawn by dawn her garden thrives,
A verdant paradise.

Until one grey dawn, she arrives
To a graveyard.
Shards of terracotta lie like splinters of broken
bone
Scattered over soil, as if it were to grow
But no
Her plants lie dead, ruined
And weeping bitter white sap
Where the stems are snapped
And crushed underfoot.
She looks over the wreckage
And stifles a scream,
Her heart breaking to see
Ripped leaves strewn about, and roots dug out
The stamped remains of her plants, once tall.
Her safe place is not so safe after all.

Madness

The patterns in the ceiling paint
Dance at the edges of your vision,
Twisting and seething,
Frothing the light into shadowy foam
Where roam
The monsters.
And the ticking on the wall
Is a portal to a world
Where a clockwork god
Grins madly down on his creators.
But now the throne stands empty,
Metal hinges rusty and creaking,
Groaning as they struggle vainly to twitch
Back into existence.
And that lingering perfume
Is the cloying scent of decay,
Thickening in your lungs like cement,
Breathless as the tomb
Of the bed where you lay.
And where you will stay,
Limbs corpse-stiff and heavy
Though your skin crawls
To get away.
And somewhere inside
A dying star flashes bright

Blinding your thoughts into static
And buzzing your mind blank
And all you can do
Is be.

The Hole

I scrabble endlessly at the sides of the pit,
Muscles corded and straining as I wail,
Fingers arthritic claws, desperate,
Dirt scratched beneath my fingernails.
I slip,
Inch by inch
As I thrash against the fall.
Sweat laughs down my spine,
Rattling in my mind,
Ropes of hair threaten to strangle.
Movement in the black,
Snickers behind my back,
As hope turns to starlight,
Forever out of reach.
I shiver with hysteria.
This Sisyphean task
Weathering me slowly away,
Until at last, panting,
I feel myself break,
And with a smile that aches
I let go.

It Begins

I choke on the umbilical noose looped around
my neck
As I scream into the world.
A shivering, mewling, pink creature
Thrust squirming into the air.
It's not fair.
I struggle and grow
And I hurt and I know,
I know now what it means to live.
Tear me sin from sin,
Break me from within,
As it begins.

The End of All Things

I stand here, at the end of all things,
Here, where I face you,
And here, where I face myself.
I'm not sure I can stand it.
This is the place we all come to alone.
A place I have always known
Was waiting in the back of my mind.
It's time, I think to myself.
My breath comes in starts,
Short and sharp,
My heartbeat the ticking
Of a running out clock,
The pounding of wardrums,
It screams at me
Stop.
I'm shaking and shivering
And begging and pleading.
Please just do it. Let it end.
I can't
I can't
My hands tremble with the effort,
But I can't make myself move.

Bleeding and screaming
I collapse in on myself
And decide to call for help.
I can't even do this right.

The Cliff Edge

On the cliff there sits a girl,
Her pale feet swing
Off the edge of the world.

She stares down her fears,
Her face is etched with salt,
From sea spray and tears.

She aches to let go,
Red eyes watch the waves,
Breaking furiously on the rocks below.

She thinks to swim,
The wind whispering in her hair,
And chilling her skin.

Stars flit against the night,
Far away, they watch coldly,
The water black in the moonlight.

She makes up her mind,
Her unquiet heart still,
As she dives.